HOW TO BE A
TOY
INFLUENCER

KAITLIN SCIRRI

Raintree is an imprint of Capstone Global Library Limited, a company incorporated in England and Wales having its registered office at 264 Banbury Road, Oxford, OX2 7DY – Registered company number: 6695582

www.raintree.co.uk
myorders@raintree.co.uk

Edited by Peter Mavrikis
Designed by Brann Garvey
Original illustrations © Capstone Global Library Limited 2022
Picture research by Morgan Walters
Production by Tori Abraham
Originated by Capstone Global Library Ltd

978 1 3982 1556 6 (hardback)
978 1 3982 1580 1 (paperback)

British Library Cataloguing in Publication Data
A full catalogue record for this book is available from the British Library.

Acknowledgements
We would like to thank the following for permission to reproduce photographs: Getty Images: Anadolu Agency, 33; iStockphoto: kate_sept2004, 38, Khosrork, 26, PeopleImages, 32, SDI Productions, 20, 27; Shutterstock: Anatoliy Karlyuk, 14, Andrey_Popov, 9, Anterovium, Cover design element throughout, art.em.po, 31, Burdun Iliya, 25, CC7, 34, David Bokuchava, 10, Dmytro Zinkevych, 44, Dragon Images, 22, GavranBoris, 17, glenda, 23, Goxy, Cover (toys), In-Finity, Cover (icon), Khakimullin Aleksandr, 8, livertoon, 43, lunamarina, 40, Monkey Business Images, 13, 15, My Life Graphic, 37, NeydtStock, 29, Olivier Le Moal, 42, Ric Caliolio Jr, 4, Sutipond Somnam, 19, Syda Productions, 6, TanyaFox, 30, Vlad_Chorniy, 16, wertinio, 36, ZikG, 11.

Every effort has been made to contact copyright holders of material reproduced in this book. Any omissions will be rectified in subsequent printings if notice is given to the publisher.

All the internet addresses (URLs) given in this book were valid at the time of going to press. However, due to the dynamic nature of the internet, some addresses may have changed, or sites may have changed or ceased to exist since publication. While the author and publisher regret any inconvenience this may cause readers, no responsibility for any such changes can be accepted by either the author or the publisher.

CONTENTS

Words in **bold** are in the glossary.

GET PAID TO PLAY!

The latest racing cars, fashion dolls and action figures fill your table. The newest Funko Pop collectibles stand in neat rows. Better yet – you didn't even have to buy any of them! You hold one of the toys to the camera for all your fans to see.

What is the hottest toy that kids will want to play with? What is the newest figure that collectors will want to own? Which toys don't live up to the hype? Thousands of people around the world have questions, and you are the person they will turn to for answers. Everyone is waiting to hear what you have to say. The stage is set, the camera is rolling and you are about to be paid to play. You are a social media toy influencer!

CHAPTER 1

WHAT IS A TOY INFLUENCER?

How does it feel to open a toy package at Christmas, your birthday or on other special occasion? It's pretty exciting, right? Toy influencers get that excitement every day!

Influencers can reach hundreds, thousands and even millions of people online through social media.

A toy influencer is someone who shares **posts**, videos and other content about toys to online **social media**. One popular type of video is called an unboxing video. In these videos, influencers open up the packaging of a toy and then play with the toy. They share all of its features. They review it and give their thoughts. Toy influencers can be any age.

CKN Toys

YouTube channel CKN Toys stars Australian brothers Calvin and Kaison. They are just 7 and 3 years old, but they have more than 15 million subscribers. Their videos have got billions of views! In 2019, Nickelodeon Australia made a deal with Calvin and Kaison to start a new television show. It's called *Calvin & Kaison's Play Power.*

Earning money

Influencers earn an **income** in different ways. One common way is through advertisements. Ads are photos or short videos that **promote** a brand or product. Influencers may place ads on their business websites or social media pages. They make money when people view or click on the ads.

A company may also pay an influencer to make a post or video for them. In it, the influencer shows off a toy the company is selling. This is called a paid post, and it's another popular way for influencers to earn.

Costs and benefits

There are **costs** and **benefits** to being an influencer. Money is both a cost and a benefit. Influencers have to spend money to get their business started. This is a cost. It could create a hardship for the influencer or their parents at first. But the influencer could earn the money back. This is a benefit. Kids like to have their own money to spend. Parents like to save money for their kids.

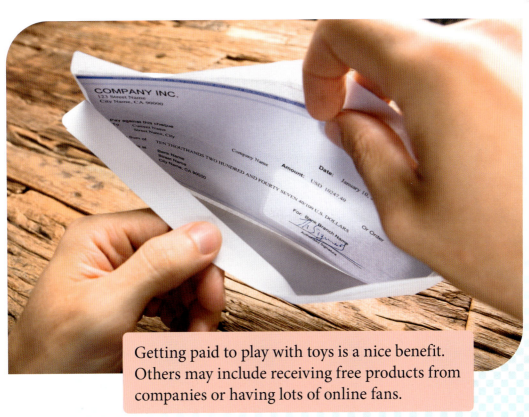

Getting paid to play with toys is a nice benefit. Others may include receiving free products from companies or having lots of online fans.

An influencer's opinions can affect which toys people decide to buy next!

Why be an influencer?

Kids like being influencers for many reasons. They get to earn money. They get access to the latest toys and collectibles. Sometimes they even get them for free.

Many people, including adults, are fans of kid influencers – or "kidfluencers". Parents like to learn which toys kids love the most. Collectors like to see the newest collectibles and hope to one day own them. Kids find unboxing videos exciting. Watching toy influencers is an escape from everyday life. They imagine what it would be like to be famous for playing with toys!

Top influencers

Influencers may focus on different topics such as fashion, gaming, music or toys. Top social media platforms used by influencers include YouTube, Twitter and Instagram. Top toy influencer YouTube accounts include Ryan's World, Kid Toy Testers and Toys and Colors.

Top toy influencers today

Ryan's World

- Influencer: Ryan Kaji (age 8)
- More than 24 million subscribers on YouTube
- More than 90,000 followers on Instagram

Some toy influencers, such as Ryan's World, become so popular that they create their own toys!

Kid Toy Testers

- Influencers: Yumiko (age 17), Sachiko (age 14), Kimiko (age 11), Kenzo (age 8), Raiden (age 5) and Takashi (age 1)
- More than 300,000 subscribers on YouTube
- More than 35,000 followers on Facebook

Toys and Colors

- Influencers: Wendy, Emma, Jannie, Alex, Andrew (ages unpublished)
- More than 20 million subscribers on YouTube
- More than 23,000 followers on Facebook

CHAPTER 2

GETTING STARTED

So you've decided to become a toy influencer. Before you start playing and reviewing for online fans, you need to set up your business.

One of the first steps is to learn about your **target audience**. This is who you want to reach. As a toy influencer, your audience will likely include kids and adults. Kids will want to learn about the toys and see what's new. Adults will want to learn about popular toys for kids. Both kids and adults are collectors and will want to see the latest in collectibles.

Fast Fact!

Top toy collectibles include Funko, Star Wars, Pokémon, Lego and Disney. These toys are popular for play but also for displaying as a collection.

Taking time to research before making videos will help set up your business for success.

You'll also want to learn all about the latest toys! Major toy company websites are a great place to start. Try looking into online stores that sell toys too. Websites such as Amazon and Argos allow shoppers to sort by newest toys. You can also read customer reviews of products.

Teamwork

A strong team can help your business succeed. Influencers may bring in a lawyer to review any legal documents. An accountant can help with the business finances. As a kidfluencer, your team must include a parent or guardian. Kids younger than the age of 18 can't start a business on their own. Your parent or guardian can sign legal paperwork for you. They can also open a business bank account. This account helps track money earned and spent on the business.

You may also want help creating videos and posts. Will someone else be in charge of filming, editing or writing? Or will you do everything yourself?

Goal setting

One of your jobs as an influencer is to decide what kind of posts to create. Do you only want to unbox and review toys? Do you want to work with all toys? Or do you want to focus on certain kinds, such as outdoor toys or retro board games? Setting clear business goals will help you keep your business on track.

Fast Fact!

In 2020, the UK toy industry made more than £3.3 billion in toy sales. The UK has the largest toy market in Europe.

Win the game by being different from other influencers!

Standing out

Influencers have a lot of **competition**. These are people who are doing the same thing as you, with the same goal in mind. Your competition is other kid toy influencers. You should look at their videos and posts. Study the most popular ones. Think about what you do and don't like about them. Then think of ways to be different. Finding a way to stand out in a crowded market will help you grow your audience.

Creating a workspace

Setting up a workspace will help keep things organized. Decide where you'll work. Will you make videos at home? Maybe you can use a basement or a garage. Or use a section of your bedroom. Make sure there's plenty of room for everything you need. Buying and using special filming and photography equipment can make your posts higher quality.

Equipment needed

- Camera for videos and photos
- Camera stabiliser
- Mobile phone
- Computer
- Editing software
- Internet connection
- Lighting kit
- Microphone
- Tripod

Setting up social media

Influencers reach others through social media, but kids may need help with online account set-up. Most social media platforms don't allow users younger than the age of 18. This includes popular toy influencer platform YouTube. But kids between 13 and 18 can sign up with help from a parent or guardian. The adult will also need to be the one in charge of account activity, such as uploading videos.

Another option is to sign up with YouTube Kids. You will still need a parent or guardian to help you sign up and they will still need to be in charge of the account. But there is no age limit for YouTube Kids.

Fast Fact!

YouTube is one of the most popular influencer platforms. It has more than 2 billion users worldwide.

Choosing a name

Some influencers use a business name instead of their real name. Try to choose one that lets people know your account is all about toys. Once you pick a name, set up social media accounts with it right away. If someone is already using the name, that's OK! Use a shortened version of the name instead. Just try to keep it the same across all your accounts.

Investments

New businesses count on **investments** to get up and running. An investment is something that goes into the business. It could be time or money. An investor is someone who puts their time or money into the business. You and your parents may invest money in the business. Friends or family members may also want to invest. Investors hope to earn their investment back and make more money once the business becomes successful.

Another option for new businesses is a loan. A loan is when a bank lets someone borrow money. If a bank loans you money, you must pay it back to the bank by a certain date. You will also have to pay extra money called **interest**. The amount of interest paid will depend on the amount of the loan. Loans should be considered carefully.

Time is an important investment too. Decide how much time to spend on influencing. Do you want to make new posts every day? Do you want to work only on the weekends? Will you step back from other activities to have time to create? Try setting a schedule. Plan time for filming and posting. This can help make sure you don't spend too much or too little time on the business.

Fast Fact!

According to a study, it takes an average of £5,000 to start a micro-business, which is a business with 10 employees or fewer.

Businesses may get into legal trouble if they don't pay taxes correctly. So it's important to keep accurate financial records.

Taxes

All businesses have to pay taxes. Taxes are money paid to the government. Even as a kidfluencer, you may have to pay taxes to the government. The amount of taxes owed depends on how much money your business makes, so it's important to carefully track your business earnings.

You should also track money spent on the business. This is called a business expense. An expense could be buying camera equipment or new toys to unbox. Business expenses can usually be subtracted from taxes, which saves you money. Ask an adult to help keep records of earnings and expenses. They should also help with taxes. Or hire an accountant.

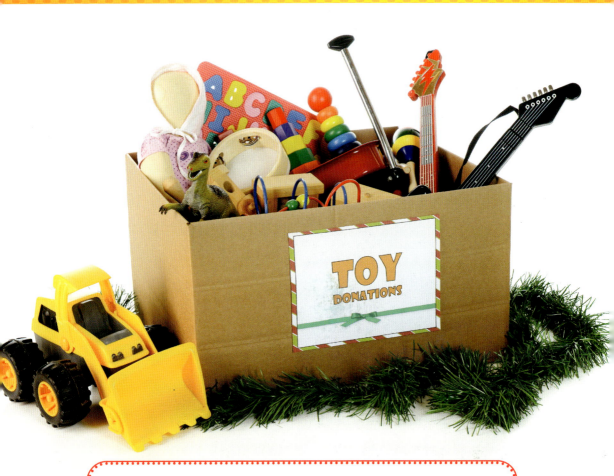

Giving back

Toy influencers review a toy, then move on to the next one. They may end up reviewing hundreds of toys. What happens to all those dolls, cars and games? Some influencers, such as Ryan Kaji of Ryan's World, donate most of their toys to charity after they've been reviewed. Charitable donations help bring joy to kids in the community. They may also be tax deductible, which helps the business' finances.

Staying safe

Influencers connect with many people online every day and sometimes they may get bullied. Someone might leave lots of nasty comments. Or someone might reach out to chat privately. You should discuss online safety with your parents or guardians. Come up with a plan on how to handle these situations. Discuss how much of your life to share. Never give out personal information such as your address or phone number.

You should also be careful with how you act online. As an influencer, your words have a type of power. So make sure you're respectful. Don't make negative comments on other users' posts. If you behave like a bully, subscribers may stop following your account. Toy companies may not want to work with you.

Bullying online is called cyberbullying, and it's not okay. Tell a trusted adult if you ever feel unsafe.

CHAPTER 3

MAKING MONEY

The business is set up. You're ready to say hello to the world and influence! In order to make money, you'll need great content that people want to watch.

Your videos should include lots of helpful info. Viewers want to know why you liked or didn't like a toy. Or why a collectible is so rare or valuable. Viewers also want to know how much the toys cost and where they can buy them. If you shopped around to find the best deal, share that too.

Mostly, viewers want to know about the toy itself. Show it from several different views. Talk about its quality. Will it stand up to lots of play or break quickly? Also mention if it needs anything additional to operate. For example, are batteries required? Maybe the toy is an action figure. Would it be okay on its own? Or would it be more fun if it was purchased with other action figures? These are all questions to think about answering in your videos.

Copyright

When creating videos, make sure you follow all laws. Many influencers have trouble with **copyright** law. A copyright protects an artist's work, such as a song. This means no one else can use it without permission. You must get permission to use copyrighted music in your videos. This includes theme songs from shows or films. It also means jingles or songs from toy commercials.

Getting copyright permission is very difficult to do. Instead, YouTube and many other social media platforms offer their own music libraries with songs and sound effects that are free to use. This is a good option if you want music in videos.

Fast Fact!

Popular video-sharing social media app TikTok uses copyrighted music. But TikTok has agreements with music companies that let users play their music in videos.

As an influencer, you may work with some of the most popular brands!

Ads, paid posts and partnerships

Influencers often earn money through ads and paid posts. Ad services let you place ads on your website and YouTube videos. Then you make money when people watch or click on the ads.

You can also earn money through paid posts. Toy companies may pay you to post about a new toy they are selling. Or a theme park might contact you. They might want you to visit their park. Then you would share pictures and videos of the park online and get paid for doing it.

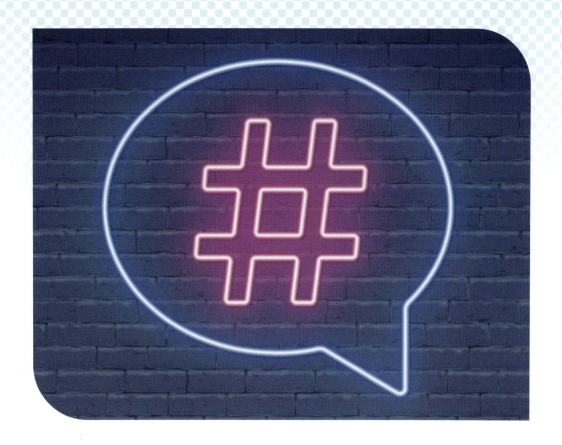

Certain laws apply to paid posts. If you agree to do one, you must follow these laws. One law says that paid posts must be clearly labelled. So you need to clearly state in your video that you're being paid to talk about the toy. You may also label the post using **hashtags**, such as #sponsored, #ad and #paidpost. Labels help viewers know the difference between paid posts and honest reviews. Viewers like to know if you are promoting a toy because you really like it or because you were paid.

Toy influencers can also make money by partnering with brand companies. That might be a kids' TV show or a shop. When you have a partnership, you place links with a special code on your website and social media pages. The links send viewers to the websites of the shops or TV shows. The special code tells the website that people found it through your link. Then the brand knows to pay you whenever someone buys something after using your link.

The YouTube Partner Program

YouTube allows influencers to make money with ads on their videos. It's called the YouTube Partner Program. People younger than age 18 are unable to apply, although an adult can apply for them. To be approved, you must have at least 1,000 subscribers and post new content often. You must also have at least 4,000 public watch hours within the previous year. Most channels need several months to meet these qualifications.

Pros and cons

As a business owner, you'll have to make many important business decisions. You should carefully study the pros and cons each time. One decision might be whether to partner with brands such as toy stores or kids' clothes shops. A pro of partnerships is earning money. You might also receive free toys or clothes to try from your partner companies. A con of partnerships could be losing followers. Some viewers only like honest toy reviews. They don't like to see products you were paid to promote.

Toy Fairs around the world

Annual toy fairs are held around the world so toy companies can showcase upcoming products. Influencers might decide to make the trip to get the scoop on what's hot.

Melbourne Toy Fair, Australia

- Held annually in February or March
- Displays the latest toys, hobby and nursery items for attendees from around the world

China Toy Expo, China

- Held annually in October
- About 20% of the products shown are educational toys and games

Nuremberg International Toy Fair, Germany

- Held annually at the end of January
- World's biggest toy fair, showing more than 1 million products

Toy Fair New York, USA

- Held annually in February
- One of the oldest fairs, with the first show held in 1903

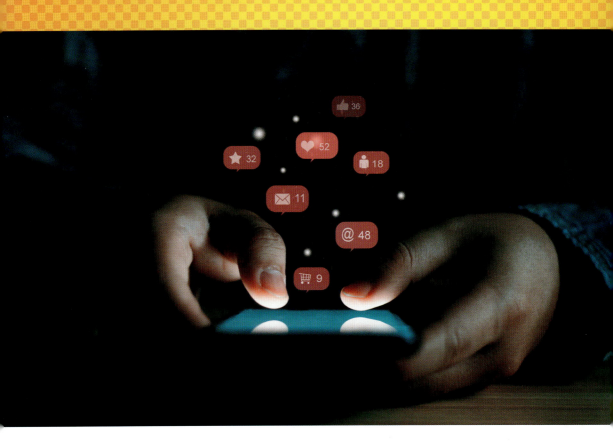

Boosting the business

Having lots of followers is good for an influencer's business. The more followers you have, the more view, clicks, likes and comments you may get on posts. This helps you earn more money! So promote your business as much as possible. When it comes to posting, don't stick with just one account. Use several! Put a video on YouTube. Then share it on Twitter or Facebook too. Using different social media sites helps reach more people.

Another way to promote the business is with a paid promotion. You pay to have your post appear in feeds. It'll show up for users who don't follow you. This can help grow your audience. But remember, paid promotions cost money. Using them is a business decision that must be thought through carefully.

Fast Fact!

The first ever TV toy advert was shown in 1952. It was for Mr Potato Head. It marked the start of using videos as paid promotions to influence toy sales.

Paid subscriptions

Some followers aren't just viewers – they are fans! Fans are sometimes willing to pay a weekly or monthly fee for extra content. This is called a paid subscription. In exchange, fans get bonuses such as extra reviews. Or maybe an early look at an upcoming video. You could also share special content such as behind-the-scenes footage. Paid subscriptions are another source of income for your business.

Working together

As a new kidfluencer, you should think about working with other influencers. You could both be toy influencers. But maybe you specialize in dolls and fashion toys. The other person focuses on action figures and racing cars. You can ask them to make crossover videos. This is when two influencers make videos together. For example, Ryan's World once worked with Japanese toy influencer The Gacchannel. They made a crossover toy video. Teaming up helped both reach more viewers in different countries.

A Family business

Many kidfluencers got started because their parents were already influencers. It's not uncommon for entire families to be influencers together or individually. Some kidfluencers develop an online following while they are still babies. Their parents set up social media accounts for them! At only 1 year old, baby influencer Halston Blake Fisher had more than half a million Instagram followers.

CHAPTER 4

GROWING YOUR BUSINESS

Your social media channel is up and running. You're having fun showcasing unique toys and gadgets – and even making some money doing it. Now what? You're ready to build to the next level!

Stakeholders

Some people have a special interest in seeing your business grow. They are stakeholders. Stakeholders might be your parents who have given their time to the business. They might be investors who gave your business money.

Stakeholders want to know your plans for the future. They like to get regular updates. They might ask about your stats – short for *statistics*. Stats include the number of views, clicks and comments on your posts. Social media sites often offer tools to track stats. For example, YouTube lets you see stats such as most popular video and average watch time. Use this info to see where you're doing well and where you can improve. Then give the update to stakeholders.

As the business owner, you are also a stakeholder. Remember to take care of yourself. Keep a regular schedule that allows enough time for rest and schoolwork. Also remember to spend time with family and friends. This is called keeping your work and personal life balanced.

New opportunities

Once you've had some success influencing, you might seek the help of an agent. An agent is someone who can help find new opportunities to grow the business. This might include helping you create your own toys to sell in shops. You might also want to create clothing for kids or appear in toy adverts on TV. An agent can guide you through this process.

Agents bring in new opportunities and can help handle the business side of influencing. In exchange, they take what's called an agent fee, typically around 10 per cent of income.

New content

Viewers and subscribers like to see new content. Influencers who have done mostly toy reviews should think about trying something new. Maybe you could post about your favourite toy shops. Or maybe you could visit amusement parks. There are also museums designed for kids. You could still focus on toys and play. But you would be exploring something different and exciting at the same time. Adding new content is a great way to keep viewers engaged while attracting new followers.

Fast Fact!

There are many toy museums for children in the UK, including the Victoria & Albert Museum for Children in London and the Museum of Childhood in Edinburgh, which is the oldest of its kind in the world.

Career paths

If you've had success with toys, you might try your influencing talents in a new area. You might talk about video games. Or maybe you'd like to share your opinions on music or fashion. You can point your subscribers to your new account. You can also point viewers of your new account back to your toy account. You could even decide to make crossover videos. These could be shared to both of your accounts.

Also look ahead to your future. Think about if you want to keep influencing. Do you want to make it a full-time career? If so, there are different subjects you can study in school that match up with skills needed for the influencing industry.

Creating careers

Fields that pair well with influencing:

- Advertising
- Business
- Economics
- Design
- Music
- Photography
- Public relations
- Social media marketing
- Videography

Future Fun

As your business becomes more successful, look for new opportunities – in and out of the industry. Maybe you'll invest in other influencers who are just starting out. Maybe you'll take your love of toys into designing new products. Influencing has endless possibilities for kids and adults who want to create a lasting career.

Now let's get started!

Timeline

1940

1950

1960

1970

1980

1990

2000

2010

2020

1950s – Companies start advertising toys in television adverts.

1957 – The first ever Toys "R" Us shop opens, in the US

1994 – Amazon.com opens for business, focusing on books but later including toys and other goods.

Early 2000s – Online reviews become popular for toys and other products as more people turn to online shopping.

2005 – YouTube launches.

2015 – YouTube channel Ryan ToysReview posts its first toy-unboxing video.

2017 – Toys "R" Us, once the number-one toy shop in the UK, files for bankruptcy.

2018 – A line of toys branded Ryan's World are sold.

2019 – The online influencer industry earns approximately £5.6 billion.

GLOSSARY

benefit something good that you gain, such as money or special gifts

competition others in the same business you are in

copyright right by law to copy, sell and publish a product or work

cost something you give in exchange for something else, such as time or money

hashtag tag to group online posts and aid in searches; it starts with #

income money someone earns or is given on a regular basis

interest charge that a borrower pays a lender

investment something, such as time or money, that is put into a cause or business

post something shared to social media, such as videos or photos

promote draw attention to something, like a business or event

social media websites people use to share content

target audience person or people the business wants to reach or sell to

FIND OUT MORE

BOOKS

Eat Sleep YouTube Repeat: a notebook for kids to get planning their YouTube empires, Louise Amodio (Beans and Joy Publishing, 2018)

Make a Movie!: Build Buzz-Worthy Video Blogs, Thomas Kingsley Troupe (Raintree, 2020)

Making YouTube Videos: Star in Your Own Video!, Nick Willoughby (For Dummies, 2019)

Understanding Social Media (Decoding Media Literacy), Pamela Dell (Raintree, 2019)

WEBSITES

influencermatchmaker.co.uk/blog/kid-influencers-meet-next-generation-social-media-stars
Find out about some of the most successful 'kidfluencers'.

www.bbc.co.uk/newsround/49822698
Read more about kidfluencers at CBBC Newsround.

INDEX